19.95

HURRICANE KATRINA

Through the Eyes of Storm Chasers

WITHDRAWN
TEMPLE PUBLIC LIBRARY

By Jim Reed and Mike Theiss

FARCOUNTRY
PRESS

Acknowledgments

JIM REED

To the memory of both my grandmother, Vivian Armstrong, and good friend Dot Degood. I miss our conversations about the weather.

Thanks to my mother, Audrey Reed, and to Katherine Bay, Jon Davies, Aaron Blaser, Mike Phelps, Joe Wasser, Greg Zamarripa, Lynn Elsey, Don Holmer, Sharon Moody, Tom and Theresa Ensign, Paul and Gail Bowen, Mike Smith, Dick Elder, Stan and Mollie Helfand, Jeff Rothberg, Joanne Wiles, Barry Tanenbaum, the great folks at Douglas Photographic, and the many dedicated scientists, forecasters, and staff at the National Hurricane Center and NOAA.

A special thanks goes out to the talented team at Farcountry Press, particularly to director of publications Kathy Springmeyer, who asked us to do the book and quickly became our literary air-traffic controller. To editor Jessica Solberg and designer Kelli Twichel, whose skill, patience, and very long hours, alongside Kathy, allowed us to create a book in near-record time. A big thank you to Terry Swails who introduced us.

Finally, a very special thanks to Mike Theiss, who did a terrific job of balancing risk-taking with safety while assisting so many Gulfport residents in the process.

MIKE THEISS

First I'd like to thank everyone I rode out the storm with for sticking together and helping each other get through this historic event. We made a great team! Thanks to Truett Martin for making arrangements for us to stay at the Holiday Inn to document Katrina from the front lines as the surge came in; United States Navy Petty Officers John Gulizia, Michael Latka, and Roger Ferris for helping us with the documentation of Katrina and for their bravery in saving Ms. Lillie Williams' life; and Jim Reed for inviting me to stay at the Holiday Inn with him and document this historic event as a team.

I'd also like to thank my mentor Jim Leonard for teaching me everything I know about hurricanes. Thanks to all my friends in the "Southside" for all the support they have given me. And last but not least, none of this would be possible if it weren't for my loving parents helping to mold me into what I am today. Mom, Dad, Kathie, and Jeff, thanks for all your support and thanks for inspiring me to fulfill my dreams in life. I love you all.

I'd like to dedicate this book to my grandfather Edward Theiss, whom I never really got to know because he died when I was one year old. He was a great photographer, and I feel he is always with me, helping and watching over me, while I'm on these extreme shoots.

ISBN 13: 978-1-56037-377-3
ISBN 10: 1-56037-377-6
© 2005 Farcountry Press
Photography © Jim Reed and Mike Theiss, unless otherwise noted
Cover photos: Top, left and right inset photos: Jim Reed;
center inset photo: Mike Theiss
Back cover photos: Top photos: Mike Theiss; bottom photo: Jim Reed
Title page photo: Mike Theiss

For more information on our books, write Farcountry Press, P.O. Box 5630,
Helena, MT 59604; call (800) 821-3874; or visit www.farcountrypress.com.

Created, produced, and designed in the United States.
Printed in Canada.

URGENT - WEATHER MESSAGE
NATIONAL WEATHER SERVICE NEW ORLEANS LA
1011 AM CDT SUN AUG 28 2005

....DEVASTATING DAMAGE EXPECTED....

HURRICANE KATRINA...A MOST POWERFUL HURRICANE WITH
UNPRECEDENTED STRENGTH...RIVALING THE INTENSITY OF HURRICANE CAMILLE OF 1969.

MOST OF THE AREA WILL BE UNINHABITABLE FOR WEEKS...PERHAPS LONGER. AT LEAST ONE HALF
OF WELL CONSTRUCTED HOMES WILL HAVE ROOF AND WALL FAILURE. ALL GABLED ROOFS WILL FAIL...
LEAVING THOSE HOMES SEVERELY DAMAGED OR DESTROYED.

THE MAJORITY OF INDUSTRIAL BUILDINGS WILL BECOME NON FUNCTIONAL. PARTIAL TO COMPLETE
WALL AND ROOF FAILURE IS EXPECTED. ALL WOOD FRAMED LOW RISING APARTMENT BUILDINGS
WILL BE DESTROYED. CONCRETE BLOCK LOW RISE APARTMENTS WILL SUSTAIN MAJOR DAMAGE...
INCLUDING SOME WALL AND ROOF FAILURE.

HIGH RISE OFFICE AND APARTMENT BUILDINGS WILL SWAY DANGEROUSLY...A FEW TO THE POINT
OF TOTAL COLLAPSE. ALL WINDOWS WILL BLOW OUT.

AIRBORNE DEBRIS WILL BE WIDESPREAD...AND MAY INCLUDE HEAVY ITEMS SUCH AS HOUSEHOLD
APPLIANCES AND EVEN LIGHT VEHICLES. SPORT UTILITY VEHICLES AND LIGHT TRUCKS WILL BE
MOVED. THE BLOWN DEBRIS WILL CREATE ADDITIONAL DESTRUCTION. PERSONS...PETS...AND LIVESTOCK
EXPOSED TO THE WINDS WILL FACE CERTAIN DEATH IF STRUCK.

POWER OUTAGES WILL LAST FOR WEEKS...AS MOST POWER POLES WILL BE DOWN AND TRANSFORMERS
DESTROYED. WATER SHORTAGES WILL MAKE HUMAN SUFFERING INCREDIBLE BY MODERN STANDARDS.

THE VAST MAJORITY OF NATIVE TREES WILL BE SNAPPED OR UPROOTED. ONLY THE HEARTIEST WILL
REMAIN STANDING...BUT BE TOTALLY DEFOLIATED. FEW CROPS WILL REMAIN. LIVESTOCK LEFT EXPOSED
TO THE WINDS WILL BE KILLED.

AN INLAND HURRICANE WIND WARNING IS ISSUED WHEN SUSTAINED WINDS NEAR HURRICANE FORCE...
OR FREQUENT GUSTS AT OR ABOVE HURRICANE FORCE...ARE CERTAIN WITHIN THE NEXT 12 TO 24 HOURS.

ONCE TROPICAL STORM AND HURRICANE FORCE WINDS ONSET...DO NOT VENTURE OUTSIDE!

*The National Weather Service
released this warning on the
morning of August 28, 2005.*

Introduction

by Jim Reed

This morning, shortly before dawn, we are abruptly awakened by silence. The hum of our hotel room air conditioner has stopped. The glow of the TV is now dark. Electricity is dead. The only sound now is that of a roaring, muffled wind on the other side of our Gulfport, Mississippi, fourth-floor hotel window.

I pull back the drapes and peer outside. The sky is a light, cool blue. Oak trees sway convulsively. Small swirling debris litters the air. Fellow severe-weather photographer Mike Theiss and I quickly check radar on a laptop computer. Seven days of forecasting and second-guessing nature have been confirmed. We're now in the direct path of Hurricane Katrina—one of the strongest storms to ever bear down on the United States.

© JIM REED

Less than twelve hours ago I was driving south on Interstate 65 beneath a sunny blue sky. On the opposite side of the road, thousands of bumper-to-bumper cars, trucks, and campers were heading north, away from the central Gulf Coast.

My cell phone rings. It's Mike, and for the first time in eight days of tracking this tropical system, he sounds edgy, even nervous. He's driving west on Interstate 10 from Pensacola, Florida, and has seen all the people driving the opposite direction. Our plan calls for meeting in Gulfport in less than two hours.

Katrina is my fifteenth hurricane interception, but every new storm brings with it a sense of apprehensiveness. Every new storm can produce surprises. Every new storm can be your last. That makes planning critical.

Mike and I have studied Katrina with excruciating care ever since the tropical cyclone's birth as a tropical depression in the southeastern Bahamas on Tuesday, August 23. By Wednesday morning, we were convinced Katrina was a significant weather story in the making and would likely make two landfalls along the U.S. coastline.

As owner of Jim Reed Photography, Severe & Unusual Weather—a science-based photo agency—I sent a dispatch to my media clients, including CNN, ABC, CBS, and NBC:

"August 24, 2005 – Quick note to let you know that for the first time since Hurricane Dennis in July, we're going into major hurricane mode here at JRP. Katrina may strike the southeast coast of FL as a Cat 1, but we're becoming increasingly concerned she may become a major hurricane once in the Gulf."

On Thursday, August 26, Mike drove from his residence in Homestead, Florida, to Fort Lauderdale and waited. As anticipated, Tropical Storm Katrina intensified into a Category 1 hurricane and slammed into the North Miami Beach area around 6:30 p.m. EDT. I provided Mike with supporting radar updates from my studio and weather lab in Columbia, South Carolina. Gusts above 90 miles per hour were measured as Katrina came ashore with blinding rain and a surprisingly strong kick. Large trees toppled, streets flooded, and many residents were left stranded without power. Eleven people lost their lives to what many were referring to as "just a Category 1" hurricane.

That night, I telephoned the beachfront Holiday Inn in Gulfport and made reservations—we needed a place to take shelter from Katrina in order to cover the hurricane in the coming days.

Having documented several tropical systems from the beachfront hotel before, I was very familiar with the building's structural integrity. Safety had been a big concern in 2002, when I was hired to lead a Twentieth Century Fox special-unit crew into hurricanes Isidore and Lili to shoot footage for the motion picture The Day After Tomorrow starring Dennis Quaid. The beachfront Holiday Inn in Gulfport served as our base of operations then, and it would be our best hope for documenting Katrina.

As I pulled into the Holiday Inn parking lot from the south shortly before 6:00 p.m. CDT on August 28, Mike's SUV bounced into the lot from the north. After traveling nearly 1,000 miles each, we literally arrived at the same time. I took that as a very good omen.

Our goal is to document Katrina's maximum winds and storm surge. Due to the rarity of our efforts, we work with numerous clients at the same time, frequently including the National Oceanic and Atmospheric Administration, television networks, and publishers of science books, encyclopedias, and dictionaries.

Mike and I spend the first part of the night unloading gear and going down our check-list: helmets, life vests, rope, first-aid kit, satellite phone, portable storm-tracking equipment, laptop with radar, flashlights, portable camping stove, water for two weeks, and food for one week.

Together we have covered more than twenty hurricanes. In 2004, we successfully penetrated the eye of all four Florida hurricanes. But this time, we are less than 100 yards from the Gulf of Mexico. We'll be documenting the storm surge of a major hurricane from very close range.

Our plan to document Katrina comes in three phases: 1) shooting while driving around the beachfront area of Gulfport in an SUV until wind gusts reach 80 miles per hour; 2) shooting from a concrete parking garage until wind gusts

© JIM EDDS

reach 100 miles per hour; and 3) shooting from the hotel during the most violent part of the storm, with wind gusts possibly exceeding 130 miles per hour.

Only eight people remain at the hotel, including Mike; me; Truett Martin (general manager); Lillie Williams (an employee of the hotel); an unidentified homeless man with two dogs; and United States Petty Officers John Gulizia, Mike Latka, and Roger Ferris, who are residing at the hotel until being transferred to a local military base. Once the storm has passed, they will be trained to operate large cranes that will be used to help construct new buildings in Iraq.

Shortly after sunrise on August 29, Mike and I step outside of the hotel to winds already in excess of 70 miles per hour, with higher gusts. It feels and looks like we're in a warm blizzard of water. Visibility is less than a quarter mile. The sky is furious.

Katrina is making landfall along the Mississippi coastline faster and earlier than expected. Most of U.S. Route 90 is already submerged. This quickly restricts the amount of time we can safely drive around in our research vehicle. Intersections have vanished beneath splashing, chaotic waves. We hear the snapping and cracking of trees. Limbs are falling.

Less than an hour after departing the parking lot, the forty-foot hotel sign comes crashing to the ground. Seconds later, a large limb comes crashing down on the rear of our vehicle, blowing out two windows. Katrina makes it clear very quickly: phases one and two will have to be aborted.

Mike and I return to the hotel and switch our focus to documenting the storm surge as it impacts the building. A fortified stairwell with access to all levels will serve as our bunker. On the third and fourth floors we have positioned blankets, flotation devices, portable lighting, water, rope, and mattresses to shield ourselves from flying debris.

During the morning hours, the three petty officers, Mike, and I rescue Ms. Williams from her first-floor guest room. As we carry her out, water rises behind us, knocking over furniture and submerging the room.

By 8:30 a.m. CDT, storm surge is pounding against the facade of the building so hard it forces water through the air conditioning vents and into the rooms. The storm surge pounds windows and walls, and the murky sea squeezes through the lobby's glass doors.

An alarm on the hotel courtesy van suddenly wails, and that's when we see it: a ten- to fifteen-foot wave heading straight for the hotel, swelling almost gently as it approaches. But we know this won't be gentle. Seconds later, the surge turns an abandoned rental car into a two-ton battering ram. The sedan pounds *against the front glass doors. Suddenly the glass shatters and the roaring surge carries the car through the lobby, forcing us into the emergency stairwell.*

Within fifteen minutes, officers of the United States Navy and two veteran hurricane chasers are humbled into an emergency bunker. The sea roars up the stairs almost animal-like, grabbing at our ankles. For more than an hour, we document the water continuing to rise, forcing us higher and higher. The first floor has disappeared beneath us.

The roaring wind makes it difficult to think, much less hear. Neighboring pieces of roof peel away. Trees pull from the ground. Surge buries an entire zip code in water and then, nearly as fast as it comes in, the water goes out. Within minutes, surge as high as the second floor recedes to less than twelve inches.

By 11:30 a.m. CDT the sky begins to lighten. Hurricane Katrina's eye is just to the west of us. Winds calm a bit, giving us time to meet as a group. Every one is safe. Scared, but safe.

Hurricane Katrina has pinned us inside the hotel for nearly nine hours, with gusts and surge peaking around 10:30 a.m. CDT. Maximum sustained wind gusts in our area are measured at between 120 and 130 mph, with an estimated storm surge of twenty-six to twenty-eight feet.

Mike and I have witnessed and carefully documented the full evolution of a major hurricane's storm surge. Now the toughest part of our job begins. Stepping outside.

The ground level of the hotel has been completely gutted. All that is left are concrete walls and protruding showerheads. Surrounding our hotel, homes and businesses have been swept away. Only concrete foundations remain. Gas lines hiss like pissed-off pythons. Where thirty-year-old trees once stood, we see only craters in the ground. Gulfport looks like an ugly new planet.

After catching our breaths, the group embraces and gives thanks. Having just photographed the landfall of the most catastrophic storm to ever strike our country, everyone at the hotel feels lucky—very lucky—to be alive.

The water level at the beach-front Gulfport Holiday Inn. Water levels reached approximately twelve feet at the hotel, which is at sixteen feet in elevation, meaning the storm surge rose to approximately twenty-six to twenty-eight feet.

The surge pushed water through the second-floor air conditioning vents, flooding the second floor.

© MIKE THEISS

The outer bands of Hurricane Katrina close in on Gulfport, Mississippi, at twilight on August 28, 2005.

© JIM REED

Piloting the jet above Hurricane Katrina.

Hurricane Hunters keep a close eye on Katrina.

Radar display showing Katrina southwest of Florida.
© JIM EDDS (ALL)

A Hurricane Hunter climbs aboard the National Oceanic and Atmospheric Administration's Gulfstream IV high-altitude jet. The researchers used the jet to study Katrina from an altitude of 41,000 feet. Dropwindsondes—devices deployed from the plane into the storm—take readings on pressure, wind components, temperature, and humidity to help forecast the track of the hurricane.

*Hurricane Katrina creates high surf as the tropical cyclone
approaches Fort Lauderdale, Florida.*

© JIM EDDS

*People stroll the beach as Hurricane Katrina nears landfall
along the southeastern Florida coastline.*

© MIKE THEISS

*Residents of Gulfport, Mississippi,
board-up windows.*

*Citizens board-up a shop in Biloxi, Mississippi,
on the afternoon of August 28.*

The Saffir-Simpson Hurricane Scale is a system of rating the intensity of hurricanes.

Category	Wind	Surge	Effects
1	74–95 mph	4–5 ft	No real damage to building structures. Damage primarily to unanchored mobile homes, shrubbery, and trees. Some damage to poorly constructed signs. Also, some coastal flooding and minor pier damage.
2	96–110 mph	6–8 ft	Some roof, door, and window damage. Considerable damage to mobile homes. Flooding damages piers. Small craft in unprotected moorings may break their moorings. Some trees blown down.
3	111–130 mph	9–12 ft	Some structural damage to small residences and buildings, minor amount of curtainwall failures. Mobile homes are destroyed. Coastal flooding destroys smaller structures and damages larger structures with floating debris. Flooding may extend well inland.
4	131–155 mph	13–18 ft	More extensive curtainwall failures, with some complete roof failures. Extensive damage to doors and windows. Shrubs, trees, and all signs are blown down. Complete destruction of mobile homes. Major erosion of beaches. Flooding may extend well inland.
5	155 mph +	18 ft +	Complete roof failure on many residences and buildings. Severe and extensive door and window damage. Some complete building failures, with small buildings swept away. Major damage to lower floors of all structures near the shoreline. Massive evacuation of residential areas may be required.

Evacuation traffic. Residents of Louisiana and Mississippi flee the path of Hurricane Katrina by driving east on Interstate 10 near Mobile, Alabama.

© JIM REED

Hurricane Katrina approaching the southeastern coast of Florida as seen from space on August 25, 2005.

Hurricane Katrina spins toward the Gulf Coast.

Hurricane Hunter pilot Lt. Mike Silah snapped this photo while flying an NOAA WP-3D Orion aircraft inside the eye of Hurricane Katrina on August 28.

Pedestrians in Fort Lauderdale, Florida, are blasted by rain, sand, and wind as Hurricane Katrina makes landfall along the southeastern coast of the United States on August 25. Despite a hurricane warning issued by the National Hurricane Center, many Floridians remained outdoors for the Category 1 tropical cyclone.

*Large waves slam into a pier near Biloxi, Mississippi, as
Hurricane Katrina approaches the Gulf Coast on August 28.*

© JIM EDDS

*Hurricane Katrina strikes near North Miami Beach with
wind gusts topping 90 mph.*

© MIKE THEISS

Trying to return to shelter, hurricane photographer Mike Theiss struggles to regain his balance during a Hurricane Katrina wind gust. Mike had ventured out a few yards for a better look at the eastern edge of Katrina's eye.

Hurricane Katrina roars into Gulfport, Mississippi, on August 29, producing whiteout conditions and destructive winds in excess of 120 mph.

© JIM REED (ALL)

U.S. Navy Petty Officer John Gulizia points to a brightening sky as the extreme eastern edge of Katrina's eye passes over the area.
© JIM REED

Hurricane photographers Jim Reed (left) and Mike Theiss document the landfall of Hurricane Katrina from the doorway of an emergency stairwell to their beachfront hotel.
© JOHN GULIZIA

Hurricane Katrina's storm surge explodes into Gulfport, Mississippi. Extreme-weather photographer Jim Reed captured this image as he photographed from the fourth-story window of a beachfront hotel, facing the Gulf. Notice how close the water is in relation to the window. Much of the second floor of the hotel was under water. The storm surge was later measured to be about twenty-eight feet high.

© JIM REED

A lone palm tree endures winds in excess of 100 mph and storm surge created by the hurricane.

Hurricane Katrina topples trees and power lines as the tropical cyclone strikes Gulfport, Mississippi.

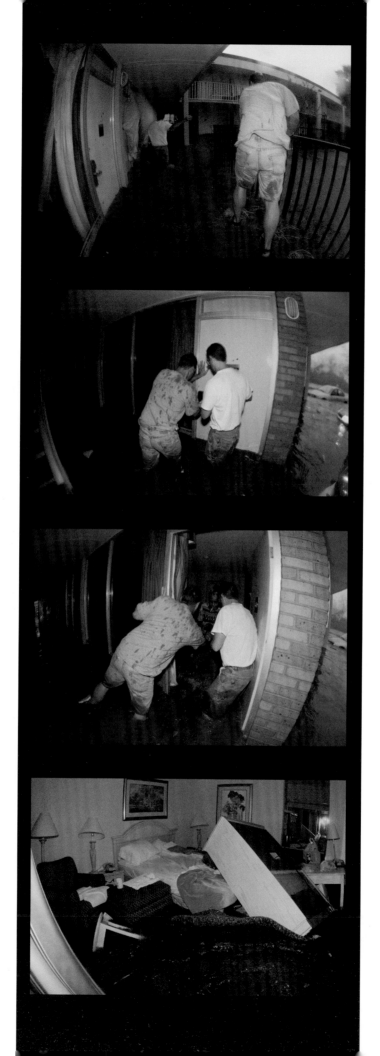

United States Navy Petty Officers John Gulizia (left) and Michael Latka rescue Lillie Williams from Hurricane Katrina's rapidly rising storm surge in Gulfport, Mississippi. Ms. Williams had been trapped inside her beachfront hotel room.

Doppler radar image showing Hurricane Katrina's eyewall about to strike the southern Mississippi coastline.

NATIONAL OCEANIC AND ATMOSPHERIC ADMINISTRATION/DEPARTMENT OF COMMERCE

Photographer Mike Theiss keeps a close eye on Hurricane Katrina's radar signature on his laptop computer from the fourth floor of a beachfront hotel in Gulfport, Mississippi. In the background, storm surge and flying debris fill the hotel's courtyard area. It should be noted that Mike spent very little time near the window and gusts were blowing away from the building. You should never be near a window during a storm.

© JIM REED

As Katrina strikes Gulfport, winds exceed 120 mph and whiteout conditions are produced along U.S. Route 90.
© JIM REED

FOR YOUR SECURITY
THIS DOOR LOCKED FROM
10:00PM TO 6:00AM
BETWEEN THESE HOURS
USE ROOM KEY CARD.

While documenting Hurricane Katrina's storm surge in a beachfront hotel parking lot, Mike Theiss is forced to take cover. This series of photographs demonstrates how fast storm surge can rise. Mike was able to safely enter the hotel seconds later.

Hurricane Katrina's devastating storm surge pours into Biloxi, Mississippi. Entire buildings and homes were blasted away by the powerful water.
© JIM EDDS

In Gulfport, Mississippi, the force of the water and wind was so strong that vehicles were swept away.
© MIKE THEISS

Hurricane Katrina's catastrophic storm surge as it roars into the lobby of a beachfront hotel in Gulfport, Mississippi, on August 29. The power of the water was so strong that it picked up cars and shoved them through the doors and into the hotel lobby. The winds and water eventually gutted the entire first floor, leaving it unrecognizable. Mike Theiss documents the rare event with United States Navy Petty Officers John Gulizia and Michael Latka. The men were forced into an emergency stairwell seconds after these photos were taken.

© JIM REED (ALL)

© JIM REED

© JIM REED

Mike Theiss documents Hurricane Katrina's storm surge as it rushes into an emergency stairwell at a beachfront hotel in Gulfport, Mississippi.

© MIKE THEISS

Prior to Hurricane Katrina making landfall, Mike Theiss positioned a remote video camera in a water-tight housing in the rear lobby of a beachfront hotel in Gulfport, Mississippi. After the hurricane had passed, Theiss retrieved the camera (above). During the height of Katrina, the camera captured never-before-seen footage of major hurricane storm surge (left). Katrina destroyed the entire first floor of the hotel.

© JIM REED

Beachfront hotel courtyard area before the landfall of Hurricane Katrina. Hotels typically place outdoor furniture into the pool to keep it from blowing away. It was a fruitless effort, given Katrina's massive force.

Beachfront hotel courtyard area during landfall of Hurricane Katrina.

AFTER

Beachfront courtyard area after Hurricane Katrina's storm surge receded.

The first floor of the beachfront Holiday Inn in Gulfport, Mississippi, was completely gutted by Katrina's storm surge.

© MIKE THEISS

Holiday Inn general manager Truett Martin takes in the severity of the damage caused by Hurricane Katrina.

© JIM REED

Aerial photograph of devastation in Gulfport, Mississippi, east of U.S. Route 49 less than twenty-four hours after Hurricane Katrina made landfall.

Katrina's storm surge obliterated entire homes and buildings.

Much of U.S Route 90 was destroyed.

estruction at the beachfront Holiday Inn hotel.

The beachfront hotel where Jim Reed and Mike Theiss documented the landfall of Hurricane Katrina. The storm

Even well-built brick homes were no match for Hurricane Katrina's crushing storm surge in Gulfport.

Jim Reed documents the devastation in Gulfport, Mississippi. In the background, residents search for their belongings.

More than two miles from the beach, many buildings and offices in downtown Gulfport, Mississippi, were destroyed or sustained heavy damage.

In Gulfport, Hurricane Katrina's ferocious winds stripped the United States Courthouse facade of several of its stone letters.

Every structure along the beachfront in Gulfport was damaged or destroyed during the landfall of Hurricane Katrina. The owner of this former condominium complex said it was one of the strongest and best-built structures in the area; yet the hurricane ravaged it.

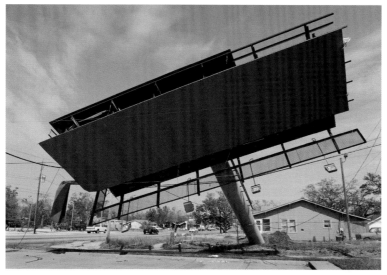

Even extra-sturdy billboards in downtown Gulfport, Mississippi, failed to survive the violent winds of Hurricane Katrina.

An industrial building in the downtown Gulfport area lies in ruins.

Katrina's storm surge wiped this beachfront Days Inn completely off of its foundation. Debris from the hotel was found more than a half a mile inland.

The streets of downtown Gulfport are buried under tons of toppled buildings and homes.

The storm surge from Hurricane Katrina displaced the Copa Casino several hundred yards from its original location.

Devastation surrounds the Grand Casino.

Employees from Marine Life Oceanarium in Gulfport try to coax two sea lions into a cage. The seas lions escaped during the landfall of Hurricane Katrina on August 29.

U.S. Route 90 is buried beneath destroyed truck trailers that were hurled about during the landfall of the hurricane.

Aerial photograph of devastation in Gulfport, Mississippi, west of U.S. Route 49 less than twenty-four hours after Hurricane Katrina made landfall.

NATIONAL OCEANIC AND ATMOSPHERIC
ADMINISTRATION/DEPARTMENT OF COMMERCE

The Entertainment Complex of the Grand Casino Gulfport sits atop U.S. Route 90 after being displaced by the storm surge. The white dashed line indicates where the building was originally located.

A resident of Gulfport, Mississippi, gestures toward the former location of the Copa Casino. The casino was blown off its foundation and moved hundreds of yards away during the explosive winds and catastrophic surge.

© JIM REED

The President Casino in Biloxi, Mississippi, was lifted out of the Gulf and displaced more than a hundred yards during the landfall.

An adult male sea lion named Elliot sits in the middle of a street next to a destroyed casino in Gulfport, Mississippi. Elliot escaped from the local Marine Life Oceanarium during Katrina's landfall on August 29. The Oceanarium was obliterated by the historic storm. Elliot was rescued shortly after this photo was taken.

© JIM REED (ALL)

Employees from Marine Life Oceanarium try to coax Elliot and another sea lion into a transport cage.

Traumatized by the hurricane, Elliot lunges at one of his rescuers.

Thousands of truck trailers were hurled inland during the landfall of Katrina.
The trailers had been parked near the port of Gulfport, Mississippi.

Much of Gulfport's beachfront was littered with tons of truck-trailer
wreckage pushed more than a quarter mile inland by storm surge.
© JIM REED (ALL)

Aerial photograph of devastation in Gulfport, Mississippi, west of U.S. Route 49, less than twenty-four hours after Hurricane Katrina made landfall.

The storm surge created by Hurricane Katrina obliterated numerous neighborhoods. The power of the wind and water was so great that entire barges and thousands of cargo containers and truck trailers were hurled more than a quarter mile inland.

Most of the beachfront hotels just west of U.S. Route 90 were wiped completely off of their foundations by the violent surge.

One of several devastated neighborhoods.

This displaced barge was pushed inland by the storm surge.

One of only a few homes left standing in the area is surrounded by tons of debris.

A grand piano lies upside down near a demolished house in Gulfport. © MIKE THEISS

The remnants of a Gulfport residence.

This mobile home, a few miles inland, was destroyed during the hurricane.

A lone microwave oven sits on a pile of sand atop what used to be U.S. Route 90 near Gulfport.

A Gulfport, Mississippi, resident looks over the devastation caused by Hurricane Katrina.

© JIM REED

Photographer Jim Reed documents the aftermath of the hurricane.

High winds produced by Hurricane Katrina, when the storm was still a Category 1, toppled this tree in Homestead, Florida.

Vehicles crushed by uprooted trees in Gulfport, Mississippi. Thankfully, no one was inside either vehicle at the time. Falling trees killed several people during Katrina's landfall in Florida.

A car lies submerged in a pool in Gulfport.

© JIM REED (ALL)

A child clutches packs of chewing gum and reacts to an off-camera police officer quickly approaching. The officer, holding a gun, was under the impression that people were looting a Gulfport, Mississippi, convenience store destroyed by the hurricane. It was soon made clear that the owner, who was also present, had given everyone permission to take whatever they wanted.

© JIM REED (ALL)

A resident of Gulfport tries to salvage belongings from his desk,
which was found in the middle of U.S. Route 90.

Photographer Jim Reed takes a break from documenting damage in Gulfport, Mississippi, on August 30. He is sitting in all that remains of a local Waffle House restaurant.

© MIKE THEISS

The storm surge of Hurricane Katrina destroyed the beachfront Waffle House restaurant, leaving only a few booths and a waffle iron behind.

© JIM REED

Katrina's high winds and violent surge moved this boat more than a quarter mile inland at Gulfport, leaving it resting against a railroad crossing.

A tangled American flag flutters in the wind the day after Hurricane Katrina's storm surge created this naturally sculpted heap of debris in the middle of U.S. Route 90 near Gulfport, Mississippi.

In 1969, Hurricane Camille pushed this tugboat out of its port in Gulf waters and well inland near Gulfport, Mississippi. The tugboat was left where it was deposited and a gift shop was built around it. The shop's sign reading "Georges Never Met Camille" refers to the approach of Hurricane Georges on September 27, 1998, when this photo was taken.

Not only did the S.S. Hurricane Camille survive Hurricane Katrina, but it remains unmoved from its location—likely because it's anchored more than three feet below the ground. Everything else around the tug, including the gift shop, was swept away.

An injured pelican tries unsuccessfully to fly while resting on floating debris in Gulfport on August 30.

*In New Orleans, a car floats in front of houses
on Canal Boulevard.*

© J. B. FORBES/ST. LOUIS POST-DISPATCH

*Katrina's aftermath in Homestead, Florida, was less
severe but did result in flooded streets.*

© MIKE THEISS

Two men walk along a washed-out road east of New Orleans on September 7.

© J. B. FORBES/ST. LOUIS POST-DISPATCH

Rescue workers from FEMA make trips back and forth from flooded Interstate 610 (background), which has been converted to a boat landing, to submerged New Orleans neighborhoods.

© J. B. FORBES/ST. LOUIS POST-DISPATCH

Much of U.S. Route 90 in Gulfport, Mississippi, is left in ruins.

© JIM REED

Photographer Mike Theiss provides a Gulfport, Mississippi, man with water and food.
Theiss and storm-chase partner Jim Reed had packed two weeks' worth of water and
a week's worth of food, which they shared with local residents. The supply was
exhausted in less than thirty hours due to demand.

© JIM REED

The National Guard arrives to check on victims at the beachfront Gulfport Holiday Inn on August 30.

© JIM REED

A pararescue team pulls a New Orleans evacuee up to a hovering HH-60 G Pavehawk on September 5.

© KELLY PRESNELL/
ARIZONA DAILY STAR

A Coastguard helicopter flies over Gulfport, Mississippi, on August 30.

© JIM REED

On September 6, sixty-nine tally marks adorn the door of a helicopter used to pluck New Orleans residents from the battered city.

© KELLY PRESNELL/ARIZONA DAILY STAR

New Orleans evacuee Connie Conway wipes away tears as she, Wayne Trepagnier, Jr., and dog Co-Co are rescued from the Crescent City on September 5.

Pararescueman technical sergeant Curtis Andes drops a case of bottled water to a few people stubbornly hanging on in the flooded streets of New Orleans.

*Two refugee dogs, Soldier (left) and Eddie, wait to be retrieved by their owner,
who was evacuated from New Orleans. The dogs, along with 180 other animals,
are sheltered at the Mississippi State Fairgrounds in Jackson by the Emergency
Animal Rescue Service.*

© ANDREW CUTRARO/ST. LOUIS POST-DISPATCH

*A volunteer coaxes a dog from its crate for some exercise at a pet shelter at the
John M. Parker Coliseum on the Louisiana State University campus in Baton
Rouge, where hundreds of pets wait to be reunited with their displaced owners.*

© KELLY PRESNELL/ARIZONA DAILY STAR

The sewer system in Gulfport, Mississippi, overflows following the landfall of the hurricane.

Thousands of transformers and utility poles were toppled and destroyed in Gulfport. More than a million people lost power in at least five states due to the massive storm.

United States Navy Petty Officers Michael Latka (far left), Roger Ferris (center), and John Gulizia hold up an American flag in front of what used to be the beachfront Holiday Inn in Gulfport. The men, who were staying at the hotel, survived the landfall of Hurricane Katrina.

© MIKE THEISS

Hurricane Katrina's massive storm surge swept a Gulfport, Mississippi, house completely off its foundation, leaving only a mangled American flag.

© JIM REED

A girl hugs her mother while the family surveys hurricane damage in Gulfport, Mississippi, on August 30.

Epilogue

by Jim Reed and Mike Theiss

The devastation that we witnessed in Gulfport was astonishing in scope, just one community in a unique region that was ravaged by massive Hurricane Katrina.

Although many people refer to Hurricane Katrina as "The Big One," meteorological evidence suggests that storms as intense, or even stronger, may occur at any time.

Every tropical depression to form in 1996 turned into a named storm, something that has never happened before in the history of the National Hurricane Center.

The 1998 Atlantic hurricane season was also historic. With fourteen named storms, ten of which became hurricanes, we witnessed one of the deadliest seasons ever recorded. In September, satellite imagery yielded the awesome, though disturbing, sight of not one, not two, not three—but four hurricanes churning across the Atlantic at the very same time. Hurricane Mitch became the strongest October hurricane ever recorded, and Nicole marked only the seventh time since 1886 that a hurricane has survived into December.

Hurricanes are now striking the United States coastline almost every year, proving that we have entered a period of increased tropical cyclone activity. Five hurricanes made landfall in 2004 alone. Many climatologists and meteorologists expect this trend to continue for several more years.

It is our hope that the images in this book will inspire people to want to learn more about our changing weather and the importance of being prepared for future storms.

Less than twenty-four hours after Katrina's catastrophic storm surge, a resident of Gulfport attaches a homemade banner to the balcony of his home, which was spared by the hurricane.

© JIM REED (ALL)

Jim Reed, 44, is emerging as one of the world's most accomplished extreme-weather photographers for his stunning images of America's changing climate. A fifteen-year veteran storm chaser, Jim has developed a skill for photographing unique storms at close-range, including tornadoes, blizzards, droughts, ice storms, lightning, and floods. He has photographed fifteen hurricanes, nine from inside the eye.

Born in Albany, Georgia, in 1961, Jim was raised in Springfield, Illinois. He then attended the University of Southern California, where he graduated with a bachelor's degree in fine arts.

Jim's career as a photographer has its roots in his childhood fascination with severe weather. In 1969, when Jim was eight years old, he and his mother unwittingly drove through the outer bands of Hurricane Camille while returning from a family vacation to Florida. By age eleven, Jim was shooting home movies of nature's wrath.

His articles and photographs have appeared in numerous books and magazines, including National Geographic, The New York Times, U.S. News & World Report, Reader's Digest and Men's Journal.

His assignments have included work for ABC's Good Morning America, CNN, Dateline NBC, Popular Science, Scientific American, Twentieth Century Fox, and Warner Brothers Pictures. He is a frequent contributor to Weatherwise Magazine.

In 2000, Jim was honored when the prestigious World Meteorological Organization commissioned four of his photographs for the agency's fiftieth anniversary calendar.

Jim has received awards from Pictures of the Year International, Photo District News, American PHOTO, and the National Weather Service. He is the recipient of the 2005 National Press Photographers Association Best of Photojournalism Award in Nature and Environment, and the 2005 MSNBC Readers' Choice Picture of the Year.

You can learn more about his current adventures and view additional images at www.jimreedphoto.com

Mike Theiss, 27, has spent nearly a decade working as a professional full-time hurricane chaser and extreme-weather photographer. He penetrated the eyewall of all four Florida hurricanes in 2004.

A native of the Florida Keys, Mike has been interested in severe weather since the age of six, when he would sit with his father on the family porch and watch the effects of thunder and lightning during summertime storms.

Mike documented his first major tropical event, Hurricane Andrew, when he was only fourteen years old. The historic storm inspired him to set his sights on studying meteorology in college, where he also studied computer graphics and filmmaking. But Mike's passion for adventure and being out in the field compelled him to take a more hands-on approach. He finished school and became the protégé of legendary hurricane-chaser Jim Leonard. Together they chased, and as months passed, Jim taught Mike the science he needed to know about intercepting nature at close range.

In 2001, Mike combined his love of weather, photography, and filmmaking and created Ultimate Chase Video Productions. His footage has appeared in scores of television specials and on networks including National Geographic Channel, NBC Dateline, CNN, The Discovery Channel, and Animal Planet. With fourteen hurricanes under his belt, he is one of The Weather Channel's most prolific contract photographers. His photographs have appeared in numerous books and magazines, including Sports Illustrated for Kids and Field & Stream.

His website, www.UltimateChase.com, is filled with fascinating information about hurricanes, tornadoes, and storm chasing. Every day, weather permitting, Mike is outside, looking up and taking pictures.